YAKALOU MEDIA

Your Perfectionism Is Killing You

Here is: How, Why and What You Need To Do

Contents

Disclaimer

This book is designed to provide information only. This information is provided and sold with the knowledge that the publisher and author do not offer any legal or other professional advice. In the case of a need for any such expertise, consult with the appropriate professional.

This book does not contain all the information available on the subject. This book has not been created to be specific to any individual's or organization's situation or needs. Every effort has been made to make this book as accurate as possible. However, there may be typographical and/or content errors. Therefore, this book should serve only as a general guide, not as the ultimate source of subject information.

This book contains information that might be dated and is intended only to educate and entertain. Regarding any loss or damage allegedly suffered or alleged to have occurred as a result of the information in this book, either directly or indirectly, the author and publisher shall have no liability or responsibility to any person or entity.

I

LET'S START HERE

Introduction

Do you ever feel like you're constantly chasing an impossible ideal? Maybe you set high standards for yourself, aiming to get everything just right, yet somehow, you still feel like you fall short. Perfectionism might seem like the key to success, but have you ever stopped to wonder if it's actually holding you back?

What if the very thing you believe will make your life better is quietly destroying it? Perfectionism often disguises itself as motivation or ambition, but in reality, it keeps you trapped in a cycle of frustration and disappointment. You work tirelessly, yet you're never satisfied, always thinking you could've done more, done better. But here's a secret many of us avoid facing: perfection is unattainable. And trying to achieve it can cost you more than you realize.

How often have you found yourself avoiding opportunities because you feared you wouldn't be good enough? Maybe you've hesitated to start a project, chase a dream, or simply take the next step in your life because it felt like the "perfect moment" hadn't come. That fear can paralyze you, and over time, it chips away at your confidence, your joy, and your potential. So, the question is—what are you really gaining by clinging to perfection?

Mistakes are not signs of failure; they're proof of progress. When you learn to let go of perfectionism, something magical happens. You begin to realize that your worth isn't tied to flawless performance or constant achievement. Instead, your growth comes from learning, from trying, and from embracing the imperfections that make you human.

This book is here to show you how perfectionism is killing your chance to thrive. By the time you're done, you'll understand how letting go of perfection is the first step toward freeing yourself emotionally, unlocking your full potential, and living a more fulfilling life. Are you ready to find out how to stop perfectionism from ruining your life?

The 5 Rules to Get the Most Out of This Book

Before you dive in, let's take a moment to think about how you can make this journey truly transformative. How many times have you read a self-help book, felt inspired, but then returned to old habits the next day? The truth is, reading alone won't change your life—it's how you approach the material and what you do with it that really counts. So, how can you ensure that this book doesn't just become another forgotten title on your shelf?

Here are five simple rules to follow that will help you get the most out of this book and start making real changes in your life.

Rule 1: Read with an Open Mind

It all begins with your mindset. You might already have beliefs about perfectionism or ideas about how to "improve" yourself. That's normal. But as you read this book, challenge yourself to be open to new perspectives. Some ideas may feel uncomfortable at first because they push against what you've always believed. Ask yourself, "What if this new way of thinking could actually help me?" Embrace the possibility that change is possible, even if it feels unfamiliar at first.

Rule 2: Take Your Time

This isn't a race. Transformation doesn't happen overnight, and neither should your approach to this book. Resist the urge to rush through the chapters, skimming over important ideas. Instead, slow down. Reflect on the concepts, and let them sink in. Give yourself the space to absorb what you're reading. After all, real growth happens when we allow ourselves time to reflect and process new information.

Rule 3: Apply What You Learn

The key to making lasting changes is action. It's easy to read about new ideas and think, "That's interesting," but if you don't apply those ideas to your life, nothing will change. So, ask yourself, "How can I use this today?" Whether it's rethinking your approach to a task or letting go of unrealistic expectations, find practical ways to put the lessons from this book into action. Small, consistent steps lead to big transformations.

Rule 4: Be Patient with Yourself

As you work through this book, remember that change takes time—and that's okay. Perfectionism has likely been part of your life for years, so don't expect to undo those patterns overnight. Be kind to yourself during this process. If you slip back into old habits, don't beat yourself up. Acknowledge the setback, learn from it, and keep moving forward. Progress isn't about being perfect; it's about showing up and trying again, even when it's hard.

Rule 5: Stay Committed

Finally, commit to seeing this journey through to the end. It's easy to start strong and lose momentum halfway through, but true transformation requires persistence. Remind yourself of why you picked up this book in the first place. What do you want to achieve? What kind of life are you working toward? Keep that vision in mind as you move through each chapter, and use it to fuel your commitment.

By following these five rules, you'll ensure that this book doesn't just inspire you temporarily but instead creates real, lasting change. It's not just about reading; it's about shifting your mindset, taking action, and being patient with the process. So, are you ready to let go of perfectionism and embrace a new way of living? Let's begin.

Word of Warning Before We Start

Before we dive in, let's pause for a moment. You've picked up this book for a reason—you want to make a change, and that's exciting. But here's something important to keep in mind: this journey isn't going to be easy. We're not just talking about surface-level tweaks; we're getting into the core of something that might be deeply ingrained in your thinking— your perfectionism. So, before we start, it's essential to know what you're getting into.

Why a warning, you ask? Because change, real change, is uncomfortable. It's natural to feel resistance. There will be moments when you'll want to close the book, walk away, and stick with what's familiar. But if you do that, you're not just walking away from the discomfort—you're walking away from growth. So, ask yourself: Are you ready to be uncomfortable if it means becoming the best version of yourself?

Here's the thing about perfectionism: it can feel like a safety net. It makes you think that if you do everything perfectly, you'll avoid mistakes, judgment, or failure. But what if I told you that perfectionism is the very thing holding you back from feeling fulfilled? Letting go of it will challenge the way you've lived for years, maybe your whole life. It will feel unfamiliar, and sometimes, it might even feel wrong. That's normal. The question is, will you trust the process long enough to see where it leads?

As we go through this book, you might feel tempted to argue with the ideas presented, to cling to the belief that perfectionism is helping you. That's your old mindset fighting back. Remember, it's okay to feel uncertain or doubtful. But here's the key: don't let those feelings stop you. Instead, ask yourself, "What if there's a better way to live, one that's not ruled by perfectionism?" Hold that thought as you move forward, even when it feels uncomfortable.

This journey is going to ask you to look closely at yourself— your habits, your thought patterns, and your fears. It's not always easy to confront these things. You might uncover truths about yourself that you didn't want to admit. But that's the first step toward freeing yourself from the chains of perfectionism. Will it be difficult? Yes. Will it be worth it? Absolutely.

So, here's the warning: if you're looking for a quick fix or an easy read, this book may not give you that. But if you're ready for an honest, transformative experience, one that challenges you and makes you grow, then you're in the right place. It's time to start the journey, knowing that it won't always be smooth, but it will lead you to a better version of yourself.

Are you ready to do the hard work? Are you willing to let go of the perfect and embrace the possible? If your answer is yes, then let's begin.

Read What You Need, When You Need It

You don't have to read this book cover to cover. In fact, the best part about this book is that it's designed to fit your life as it is right now. If you're feeling overwhelmed today, there's no need to power through every chapter in order. Instead, take a moment to reflect on what you need most at this moment. This book isn't a strict journey but a flexible guide that adjusts to where you are emotionally and mentally.

Maybe you're struggling with procrastination or beating yourself up over a small mistake. Flip to the section that deals with these topics, and dive in. Why read through pages that don't speak to you at this time when you can get straight to the advice or insight that will make the biggest difference today? It's okay to skip around, because perfection isn't required here— just progress.

This isn't a race, nor is it a test. Each chapter is written to stand on its own, so you won't miss anything by jumping ahead or moving around the book. The questions at the end of each section are there to help you think, reflect, and apply what you've read to your life right now. Don't feel pressured to answer every single one. Pick the ones that resonate with you, the ones that spark something inside.

So, go ahead—flip through the pages, find the sections that speak to you, and let your curiosity guide the way. The goal here is not to finish the book as fast as possible, but to find the wisdom that's most useful for where you are in your journey today.

II

HERE IS: HOW, WHY AND WHAT YOU NEED TO DO

Chapter 1: Fear of Failure

Perfectionism and fear of failure go together like peanut butter and jelly—except way less tasty and far more stressful. If you've ever avoided trying something new because you were worried it wouldn't turn out perfectly, then you know exactly what I'm talking about. It's that nagging little voice in your head that says, "If it's not flawless, don't bother." But here's the real question: What if it *doesn't* have to be flawless?

Think about it. How many times have you dodged a challenge or put off something you were excited about just because you couldn't guarantee a perfect result? Maybe you've always wanted to learn to play the guitar, but the thought of fumbling through a few awkward chords in front of people made you stick to air guitar. Or perhaps you've dreamt of starting a business, but the fear of not getting everything *just right* on day one left your plans stuck in dreamland. Sound familiar?

Fear of failure loves to disguise itself as perfectionism. It's sneaky like that. It makes you think that you're being responsible, cautious, or even smart by waiting until you're fully prepared. But the truth? Perfectionism isn't helping you avoid failure—it's helping you avoid *starting*. And that's worse, isn't it? Because when you never even begin, you fail by default. Ouch, right?

Here's the funny part (well, funny in a "laugh at ourselves" kind of way): The fear of failure actually guarantees the thing you fear the most! How ironic is that? By trying so hard to avoid mistakes, we make the biggest mistake of all—missing out. No one gets it perfect the first time. Imagine if babies gave up on walking after their first stumble. Ridiculous, right? We'd all still be crawling around, frustrated but too stubborn to fall down again.

But as adults, we forget that. We get so attached to the idea of success being neat and tidy that we forget that falling flat on our faces is how we learn to stand tall. So what if you don't do it perfectly the first time—or the second, or the third? That's kind of the point! Each stumble is a step closer to success. What's more, failure isn't the opposite of success; it's part of the process. I mean, what would a good success story be without a few bumps along the way?

Now, let's not pretend that failure doesn't sting sometimes. Of course, it does. No one enjoys a bruised ego. But here's a little secret: perfectionists often fear failure not because it's truly awful but because of what it *feels* like. The discomfort, the embarrassment, the "what will they think?" whispers in our heads. But when you peel back those layers, what's left? A lesson. And that's what failure really is—a little rough around the edges, sure, but always full of lessons you can't get any other way.

So what's the solution to this fear of failure? Stop treating failure like a dirty word. Instead, think of it as a passport stamp on your journey. No one travels the world without a few stamps in their passport, and no one grows without a few failures to their name. If you're not failing every once in a while, you're playing it way too safe—and that's no way to reach your potential.

Here's something else to consider: What would happen if you *did* fail? Not hypothetically, but really think about it. What's the worst that could happen? You might feel a little embarrassed, sure. But will the world end? Will people laugh at you forever? Probably not. In fact, most people are too busy worrying about their own lives to pay much attention to your failures. And the few who do notice? They'll probably respect you more for having the guts to try in the first place. Courage is contagious.

So, why not take that leap? Sure, you might fall. But what if you soar?

Reflection Questions:

1. What is one thing you've always wanted to try but haven't because you were afraid of failing?
2. How would your life change if you let go of the need to be perfect?
3. When was the last time you took a risk and it didn't go as planned? What did you learn from it?
4. What's the worst that could happen if you tried something new and didn't succeed?
5. How do you react when you see other people fail? Do you judge them as harshly as you judge yourself?

Practical Exercise:

Pick something small that you've been avoiding because you're afraid you won't do it perfectly. It could be anything—a hobby, a task at work, or even a conversation. Set a timer for 15 minutes and give it your best shot, without worrying about the outcome. At the end of the 15 minutes, reflect on how it felt to take action, even if it wasn't perfect.

Remember, progress beats perfection every time.

Chapter 2: Procrastination

Ah, procrastination. The arch-nemesis of productivity and the best friend of perfectionism. If you've ever told yourself, "I'll start when things are just right," then you know exactly how these two love to conspire against you. Waiting for the "perfect" time to start a task? That's like waiting for a unicorn to show up at your front door with a pizza and a winning lottery ticket— pretty unlikely.

But seriously, have you ever caught yourself doing everything *except* what you're supposed to be doing? You've got that big report due, but suddenly you're an expert on organizing your sock drawer or Googling "how to fold a fitted sheet." (Side note: Does anyone really know how to do that? It seems impossible!) The point is, we've all been there. Procrastination feels safe. It's cozy. It lets you avoid the messy reality of starting something that might not be perfect.

But let's ask the obvious question here: When *is* the perfect time? If you're waiting for the stars to align, for your energy to peak, or for life to just magically hand you a clear schedule with zero distractions, you're going to be waiting a *long* time. Perfectionists often tell themselves, "I'm not procrastinating; I'm just waiting until I'm fully prepared." But let's be real—how often does that moment of full readiness actually arrive? Spoiler alert: almost never.

Procrastination is like quicksand. The longer you stand in it, the deeper you sink. You convince yourself that you're being responsible, planning everything down to the last detail, but in reality, you're just spinning your wheels. The task sits there, growing bigger and scarier the more you delay. And guess what? The more you wait, the harder it feels to start. It's like trying to jump into a moving train—every second you hesitate, it gets faster and scarier.

But why do we procrastinate so much? The simple answer is: fear. Not the dramatic, run-out-of-a-haunted-house kind of fear, but a sneaky, quieter fear. The fear of not doing something perfectly. The fear of starting and realizing, "Hey, I'm not as good at this as I thought." So, you put it off. You tell yourself you'll start later, when you're *really* ready, when things calm down, when you're feeling more inspired. Sound familiar?

Here's the funny thing about procrastination: it's exhausting. You might think you're resting or taking a break by not starting, but mentally, you're wearing yourself out. The task you're avoiding doesn't go away. It sits there, lurking in the back of your mind, reminding you every so often, "Hey, remember me? I'm still here, and I'm not going anywhere." Even when you're not actively working, your brain is busy playing mental dodgeball, trying to avoid the task. No wonder you feel drained!

Let's break this down: If you procrastinate because you fear not being perfect, you're setting yourself up for a never-ending loop. You wait, hoping the perfect moment will come, but it doesn't. Meanwhile, the pressure builds, and suddenly, a small task feels like climbing Everest. But here's the thing—once you start, it's never as bad as you imagined, right? The hardest part is always the first step. After that, it's like coasting downhill on a bike. You just have to get moving.

So how do you beat procrastination? Stop making "perfect" the goal. Instead of waiting for ideal conditions, focus on just starting—no matter how small the first step is. Break the task down into bite-sized pieces and commit to completing just one piece. Once you're in motion, things tend to fall into place. And even if they don't go perfectly, at least you're making progress, which is more than you can say for procrastination. Progress, even messy progress, is always better than sitting on the sidelines, waiting.

Picture this: You've been meaning to paint your bedroom for months, but you keep putting it off. You tell yourself you'll start when you have a whole weekend free, when the weather's right, or when Mercury isn't in retrograde. But what if, instead of waiting for that perfect weekend, you just grabbed a brush and painted *one* wall? Sure, the room won't be done, but it's a start! And guess what? That one wall will probably motivate you to finish the rest. That's the magic of starting—it creates momentum.

At the end of the day, perfectionism and procrastination are two sides of the same coin. Both are rooted in the fear of not being good enough. But here's the kicker: doing something imperfectly is always better than doing nothing perfectly. Life isn't about waiting for the perfect moment; it's about making the most of the moments you have. And those moments are happening *right now*.

Reflection Questions:

1. What's one thing you've been putting off because you're waiting for the "perfect" time?
2. How would it feel to take one small step toward that task, even if it's not perfect?
3. When have you procrastinated in the past, and how did it make the task harder than it needed to be?
4. What's more important to you: making progress or waiting for perfection?
5. How does procrastination affect your mood and energy levels?

Practical Exercise:

Choose a task you've been putting off. Set a timer for 10 minutes, and commit to working on it—just for those 10 minutes. Don't worry about finishing it or doing it perfectly. Just start. After 10 minutes, stop and reflect on how it felt to take action, even if it wasn't perfect.

Remember, waiting for the perfect time is like waiting for a bus that's never going to show up. It's time to start walking.

Chapter 3: Missed Opportunities

Picture this: you're standing at a crossroads, one path leading to a safe, familiar place where everything is under control, and the other winding into uncharted territory, full of possibilities, but also… risks. You could grow, learn, and discover new things, or you could trip up, stumble, and—gasp—make mistakes. Which way do you choose? If perfectionism is your guide, you're probably sticking to the safe road. But here's the problem: that safe road? It's a dead end.

How many opportunities have you let slip by because they didn't come wrapped in the neat little package you imagined? Maybe you passed on a new job because it wasn't *exactly* what you wanted, or skipped out on a creative project because you weren't sure you'd nail it perfectly. It's easy to do. Perfectionism tells us that if something isn't flawless—or if we aren't *sure* we can be flawless—then it's better not to do it at all. But here's a little secret: that's how you miss out on some of the best things in life.

Let's be honest, life isn't a perfectly wrapped gift that arrives exactly how and when you expect it. It's more like a mystery grab bag at a yard sale—you never quite know what you're going to get, but that's part of the fun! Waiting for things to be perfect before you dive in is like standing in front of a buffet and saying, "I'll eat once everything looks perfect." By the time you decide, all the good stuff is gone, and you're left with wilted salad. Missed opportunities work the same way—they disappear while you're busy waiting for perfect conditions.

Why do we do this to ourselves? It's simple: we equate imperfection with failure. And no one wants to fail. But what if we flipped that thinking? What if we saw imperfection as part of the journey, not something to avoid? The truth is, growth often comes from stepping into situations that *aren't* perfect, because those are the situations that push us. It's in the messiness, the mistakes, and the risks that we find out what we're really capable of.

Think about this: Have you ever met someone who seems to have endless stories about cool things they've done—new jobs, spontaneous trips, side projects? Do you think those people were perfectly prepared for every opportunity that came their way? No way! They just jumped in. They didn't let the fear of imperfection stop them from saying "yes" to new experiences. And because of that, they've grown, learned, and collected some pretty great stories along the way.

Now, here's where perfectionism really does a number on us: it convinces us that the missed opportunity isn't such a big deal. You tell yourself, "Oh, that wasn't really for me," or, "I'll get another chance when I'm better prepared." But deep down, you know that's not true. Sometimes, opportunities come along once and never again. That workshop you didn't attend? That chance meeting you passed on? Those were doors that could've led to something new and exciting—but they're closed now. Sure, other doors might open, but how long will you keep closing them before you realize you're the one locking yourself out?

The funny thing is, we often think that taking risks and making mistakes will make us look bad or seem less capable. But in reality, people tend to admire those who take chances. When you try something new, even if you fumble, it shows courage. It shows that you're willing to learn, to grow, to step outside of your comfort zone. And, let's face it, people who stay in their comfort zone don't have nearly as much fun.

Here's a story to chew on: Imagine you've always wanted to try public speaking. You finally get invited to give a talk at a small event, but you're not 100% ready, and the idea of messing up in front of people terrifies you. So, what do you do? If you're aiming for perfection, you probably turn it down, telling yourself you'll say yes next time when you're "more prepared." But will you ever feel *perfectly* prepared? Nope. What you've really done is let the chance to grow and improve slip right through your fingers. You missed an opportunity, not because you weren't capable, but because you were waiting for some magical moment when perfection would just appear.

The truth is, opportunities are like shooting stars—they show up unexpectedly, they don't last long, and if you're too busy hesitating, they're gone before you even realize it. Sure, some risks might not turn out perfectly, but the growth you gain from saying "yes" far outweighs the comfort of saying "no." Life isn't meant to be lived with the brakes on, waiting for everything to feel safe and flawless. Sometimes, you just have to hit the gas and see where the road takes you.

The next time an opportunity comes your way, ask yourself: Am I saying no because I'm truly not interested, or because I'm afraid I won't do it perfectly? If it's the latter, maybe it's time to take the plunge and embrace the possibility of imperfection. You might just surprise yourself with what you can do when you let go of the need to be perfect.

Reflection Questions:

1. Can you think of an opportunity you missed because you were afraid it wouldn't go perfectly? How do you feel about it now?
2. What's the worst that could happen if you said "yes" to an opportunity, even if you weren't fully prepared?
3. How does waiting for perfection prevent you from trying new things?
4. Do you admire others who take risks, even if they're not perfect? What do you admire about them?
5. What would it feel like to take a chance on an opportunity, knowing that imperfection is part of the process?

Practical Exercise:

Identify one opportunity you've passed on recently because of perfectionism. Reach out, revisit it, or find a similar one and commit to saying "yes," even if the conditions aren't perfect. Afterward, reflect on how it felt to take that step and what you learned from the experience.

Remember, the best stories don't come from playing it safe—they come from embracing the unknown. Let those opportunities in, even if they don't come with guarantees.

Chapter 4: Lower Self-Esteem

Let's talk about self-esteem. You know, that little voice inside your head that says, "Hey, you've got this!" or sometimes, "What were you thinking? You're terrible at this!" If you're a perfectionist, you might be a little too familiar with that second voice. Setting sky-high standards and constantly feeling like you don't measure up? Yeah, that's a recipe for feeling like you're not good enough, even when you're more than capable.

Have you ever felt like no matter how much effort you put into something, it's never quite good enough? Maybe you finally finish that project at work, but instead of celebrating, you obsess over the tiniest details that could've been better. Or you've worked hard on a personal goal, but once you reach it, you barely take a moment to acknowledge your achievement before moving the bar even higher. Sound familiar? It's like you're running a marathon where the finish line keeps moving further away. Exhausting, right?

Here's the thing about perfectionism: it makes sure that no matter how much you achieve, you're always left feeling inadequate. When your standards are unattainably high, you set yourself up for failure before you even begin. It's a sneaky trap. You tell yourself, "If I just do everything perfectly, I'll feel great about myself!" But perfection never comes, and instead of feeling proud, you feel like you've fallen short. Again.

It's no wonder that perfectionism and low self-esteem are best buddies. Constantly aiming for impossible standards is like setting yourself up to lose a game where you make all the rules—but the rules are so tough, even *you* can't win. And the more you fall short, the more that voice inside your head starts whispering things like, "You're not good enough," "You'll never measure up," or "Why even bother trying?"

The worst part? Perfectionists often believe that the key to feeling better about themselves is to just be *more* perfect. If they can just work harder, do more, and achieve that elusive flawless result, then maybe—just maybe—they'll finally feel good about themselves. But here's the truth: chasing perfection is like chasing a mirage in the desert. It's always out of reach, and the more you chase, the thirstier you get for validation that never comes.

Now, let's take a step back and look at this logically. If you're constantly setting yourself up for failure, how can you ever expect to build self-esteem? Imagine telling a friend, "You're not allowed to feel good about yourself until you're perfect." Sounds pretty harsh, right? But perfectionists say this to themselves all the time! The problem is, it's not perfection that builds self-esteem; it's accepting your imperfections and recognizing your worth *despite* them.

Here's a fun fact: people with healthy self-esteem are not the ones who never make mistakes or always hit their goals. Nope. They're the ones who are okay with not being perfect. They've figured out that it's not about doing everything flawlessly; it's about valuing themselves *whether* or not things go perfectly. Self-esteem isn't earned by ticking off a list of perfect achieve-ments. It's built by knowing that you're worthy, imperfections and all.

But how do you get there if you've spent years telling yourself that perfection is the only way to feel good about yourself? First, you need to start noticing when you're setting yourself up for a fall. The next time you find yourself thinking, "If I don't get this just right, I'm a failure," pause and ask yourself: is that true? Would you judge a friend that harshly if they were in your shoes? Probably not. So why do it to yourself?

Another thing to keep in mind is that no one, and I mean *no one*, is perfect. Not even that person you admire who seems to have it all together. They have flaws, they make mistakes, and guess what? They're still worthy of love, respect, and success—just like you. Lowering your impossible high standards doesn't mean lowering your self-worth. In fact, it's quite the opposite. When you allow yourself to be human (because spoiler: you *are* human), you give yourself permission to feel good about your efforts, even if they aren't perfect.

Think about this: would you rather feel constantly stressed and inadequate because you're not reaching some unrealistic version of "perfect," or would you prefer to feel good about the progress you're making—even when it's messy? It's kind of like choosing between running a race where you're tripping over your own shoelaces or walking at your own pace, enjoying the scenery. One way leads to exhaustion and disappointment, the other to a healthier, more positive sense of self.

And here's the best part: once you stop demanding perfection from yourself, you'll start to notice that you're *more* confident. When you know that you don't have to be flawless to be valuable, you can approach challenges with less fear and more courage. Suddenly, that little voice in your head saying, "You're not good enough," starts to get quieter, and a new voice takes its place—

the one that says, "You're doing great, just as you are."

Reflection Questions:

1. When have you set an unrealistically high standard for yourself and felt disappointed afterward? How did that affect your self-esteem?
2. How would it feel to celebrate progress instead of perfection?
3. In what areas of your life do you feel like you're constantly falling short, even when you're giving it your all?
4. How do you treat yourself when you make a mistake? Is it different from how you treat others when they make mistakes?
5. What would change in your life if you believed that being "good enough" is truly enough?

Practical Exercise:

Pick one task or goal this week and intentionally set a more realistic standard for it. For example, if you usually aim to finish something flawlessly, set a goal to complete it to the best of your ability without worrying about perfection. Afterward, reflect on how it felt to achieve a more realistic goal and how it impacted your sense of self-worth.

Remember, building self-esteem isn't about proving you're perfect—it's about realizing you don't have to be. You're already enough, just as you are.

Chapter 5: Increased Anxiety

Let's talk about anxiety. That tight feeling in your chest, the racing thoughts, the sweaty palms. Sound familiar? If you're a perfectionist, anxiety might be your constant companion. It doesn't just stroll in now and then—it moves in, unpacks its bags, and gets comfy. Why? Because when you're chasing impossible standards, the stakes always feel sky-high. And when things don't go according to plan (spoiler alert: they rarely do), it can send your stress levels through the roof.

Imagine this: You've got an important project, and your perfectionist brain is telling you it has to be flawless. You're visualizing every tiny detail, from the font size to the color scheme, and anything less than perfect feels like a disaster waiting to happen. Your mind races with "what ifs." What if I mess up? What if people notice? What if it's not good enough? Before you've even started, you're wound up tighter than a drum. Sound familiar? It's the perfectionism-anxiety tango, and it's exhausting.

Perfectionism has a way of turning everyday tasks into high-pressure events. Something as simple as sending an email can feel like a make-or-break moment. You reread it 17 times, making sure every word is just right, afraid to hit send in case there's a tiny error. Or maybe you've got a presentation to give, and you're so fixated on nailing every point perfectly that your stomach is in knots for days leading up to it. The more you strive for perfection, the more anxious you become about not achieving it.

Here's the frustrating part: Perfectionism convinces you that if you work hard enough, plan meticulously, and control every detail, you can avoid mistakes and, therefore, avoid anxiety. But that's a trap. Because life isn't perfect, and things don't always go according to plan. And when they don't, that anxiety you were trying to avoid? It comes crashing in like a tidal wave. You've set yourself up to feel like a failure, not because you actually failed, but because you set a standard no one could meet—not even you.

So, let's get to the heart of it: Why does perfectionism cause so much anxiety? The answer is pretty simple. When you demand perfection from yourself, you're living in a state of constant tension. There's no room for flexibility, no margin for error, no space to relax. Every little hiccup feels like a catastrophe, every misstep feels like a reflection of your worth. And the result? You're always on edge, always worrying about what could go wrong, because perfection leaves no room for mistakes.

Anxiety, in this context, isn't just an occasional visitor— it's the background noise of your life. The more you demand perfection, the louder that noise becomes. You might feel it physically (hello, headaches, stomach issues, and sleepless nights), mentally (endless loops of worry and self-doubt), and emotionally (feeling overwhelmed, irritable, or even panicked). The pressure to be perfect becomes overwhelming, and instead of motivating you to do your best, it paralyzes you.

But here's the good news: You don't have to live like this. Anxiety doesn't have to be your constant companion. The key is understanding that perfection isn't the solution to anxiety—it's the cause. The more you chase it, the more anxious you become. It's like running on a treadmill set to the highest speed, and no matter how fast you go, you can't keep up. Eventually, you're going to wear yourself out.

What would happen if you gave yourself permission to be *imperfect*? What if you could finish a task without obsessing over every tiny detail? What if you could mess up, laugh it off, and move on? Here's a little secret: People who aren't perfectionists make mistakes all the time—and they survive. They don't crumble under the weight of anxiety because they understand that mistakes are part of the process. They give themselves grace, something perfectionists rarely do.

Let's put this into perspective. Picture an artist painting a canvas. If they were a perfectionist, they might agonize over every brushstroke, terrified that one wrong move would ruin the entire painting. But most great artists don't do that. They understand that sometimes a "mistake" becomes part of the masterpiece. They go with the flow, adjust, and keep creating. Life is like that painting. If you're too focused on getting everything just right, you miss out on the beauty of the bigger picture.

And here's the irony: Perfectionism doesn't actually lead to perfection. It leads to burnout, anxiety, and a constant feeling of not being good enough. So, why keep striving for something that only makes you feel worse? What if you could lower the stakes? What if, instead of aiming for perfection, you aimed for progress, growth, or simply doing your best? The weight of anxiety would start to lift, because the pressure wouldn't be so intense. You'd give yourself room to breathe.

It's time to challenge that anxious voice in your head that tells you perfection is the only option. Start asking yourself: What's the worst that could happen if things aren't perfect? Will the world end if you make a mistake? Probably not. In fact, the world is much more forgiving than your perfectionist brain would have you believe. And here's a fun fact: people often admire those who are open about their imperfections, because it makes them *relatable*. No one connects with perfect—they connect with real.

So, let's make a deal. The next time you feel anxiety creeping in because something isn't going perfectly, remind yourself that it's okay to let go. Give yourself permission to do things "well enough" instead of perfectly. Take a deep breath, embrace the messiness of life, and know that by doing so, you're not just reducing your anxiety—you're actually giving yourself the freedom to grow and thrive.

Reflection Questions:

1. What are some situations where you feel the most anxious about being perfect? How does that anxiety affect your ability to enjoy the process?
2. How does striving for perfection create more stress in your day-to-day life?
3. What would happen if you allowed yourself to do something "well enough" instead of perfectly? How would that change your feelings of anxiety?
4. Can you think of a time when a mistake turned out to be a valuable learning experience?
5. How do you feel physically and emotionally when perfectionist pressures increase your anxiety?

Practical Exercise:

Choose a task or project that usually triggers your perfectionist tendencies. This time, set a realistic goal—one that doesn't require perfection but focuses on simply getting it done. As you work, remind yourself that it's okay if it's not flawless. After completing the task, reflect on how letting go of perfection impacted your anxiety levels.

Remember, life is messy, and that's okay. The less pressure you put on yourself to be perfect, the more space you create for joy, creativity, and—most importantly—peace.

Chapter 6: Difficulty with Relationships

Let's face it: relationships are hard enough without adding perfectionism into the mix. But for a perfectionist, relationships can feel like a minefield. Why? Because when you expect yourself to be perfect, it's all too easy to expect the same from everyone else. Suddenly, the people around you aren't just friends, family, or partners—they're potential sources of disappointment when they (inevitably) fall short of your sky-high expectations.

Think about it. Have you ever gotten frustrated because someone didn't meet your standards? Maybe your friend didn't organize your birthday party exactly the way you would've done it. Or perhaps your partner didn't say the "perfect" thing when you were upset. Instead of appreciating their effort, you zeroed in on what they didn't do right. It's easy to slip into this mindset when you're a perfectionist—after all, if *you're* striving for perfection, shouldn't everyone else be doing the same?

Here's the problem: No one is perfect. (Shocking, I know.) And expecting perfection from the people in your life is a one-way ticket to strained relationships. Perfectionism creates a gap between reality and expectation, and when people don't measure up, it can feel like a personal betrayal. "How could they let me down like that?" you think. But here's the thing—most of the time, they're not letting you down. They're just being human, with all the flaws, quirks, and differences that come with it.

Now, let's talk about how this affects the people around you. Imagine constantly feeling like you're walking on eggshells around someone, afraid that you'll never be able to meet their standards. Not fun, right? That's how your loved ones might feel when your perfectionism spills over into your relationships. They start to worry that no matter what they do, it won't be good enough for you. And let's be honest, no one likes feeling that way.

Perfectionism in relationships can look a lot like nitpicking. You focus on tiny flaws and mistakes, and before you know it, those small things overshadow everything else. Maybe your partner doesn't load the dishwasher the "right" way, or your coworker didn't handle a project exactly as you would have. It's tempting to jump in and fix things, but here's the catch: when you're constantly correcting others or pointing out what they did wrong, it sends the message that they can't do anything right.

And what happens next? Resentment. Slowly but surely, people start to pull away. They might feel judged, unappreciated, or like they can never win. And who could blame them? Perfectionism puts pressure on your relationships, making it harder for you to connect with people on a deeper level. Instead of focusing on the positives and accepting the occasional flaws, you're stuck in a loop of frustration, constantly wishing others could meet your unattainable standards.

But here's a question for you: What's more important— having a perfect relationship or having a *real* relationship? Spoiler: you can't have both. Real relationships are messy. People make mistakes, say the wrong thing, and sometimes forget important dates. But they also bring joy, support, laughter, and love. By demanding perfection, you risk missing out on those beautiful, imperfect moments that make relationships worthwhile.

Let's dive deeper into what's really going on here. Perfectionism in relationships often stems from the same place as personal perfectionism: fear. Fear of vulnerability, fear of being hurt, and fear of things not turning out "right." It's like you're trying to control the people around you so you can feel safe and secure. But here's the thing—you can't control other people, no matter how hard you try. And constantly holding them to impossible standards is a recipe for disappointment—for both of you.

So, how do you break the cycle? Start by embracing the idea that people's differences and flaws are what make them special. Your best friend might be terrible at planning, but she's always there to listen when you need to vent. Your partner might not have a way with words, but their actions show you how much they care. When you let go of the need for everyone to do things perfectly, you open yourself up to appreciating who they truly are, flaws and all.

Here's a fun little exercise: The next time someone does something that irritates your perfectionist side, pause and ask yourself, "Does this really matter?" If the answer is no (and it usually is), take a deep breath and let it go. People aren't going to meet your standards all the time, and that's okay. What's more important is the love, support, and connection you share—not whether they remembered to fold the towels just right.

Another thing to consider: perfectionism can make you less open to receiving help or support from others. If you're constantly worried that no one else can do things as well as you, you'll start to take on everything yourself. But relationships are built on give and take. When you allow people to help, even if they don't do it perfectly, you're showing trust. And that trust strengthens your bond with them.

Here's the takeaway: Perfectionism is a relationship road-block. It prevents you from fully connecting with others because you're too focused on what's wrong. But when you lower those impossible standards and allow people to be their wonderfully imperfect selves, you'll find that your relationships become richer, deeper, and more fulfilling. And guess what? You'll be a lot happier, too.

Reflection Questions:

1. Can you think of a time when your perfectionism caused tension in a relationship? How did that make the other person feel?
2. What expectations do you place on the people closest to you, and are they realistic?
3. How would your relationships change if you focused more on appreciating people's strengths rather than their flaws?
4. How do you feel when someone criticizes or nitpicks you? Do you unintentionally do the same to others?
5. What would happen if you let go of the need for your relationships to be perfect and accepted them for what they are?

Practical Exercise:

This week, when someone close to you does something that irritates your perfectionist tendencies (like loading the dishwasher the "wrong" way or forgetting a small detail), practice letting it go. Focus on the bigger picture—what they do right, how they support you, and what you value about the relationship. At the end of the week, reflect on how letting go of small imperfections affected your interactions.

Remember, people aren't perfect—but that's what makes relationships so wonderfully unique. When you embrace the beauty in imperfection, you allow your relationships to grow stronger and more authentic.

Chapter 7: Burnout

Ah, burnout—the dreaded word no one wants to hear but so many of us have felt. It's that point where you're so mentally, physically, and emotionally drained that even the thought of doing something makes you want to hide under a blanket and never come out. And if you're a perfectionist, burnout isn't just a distant possibility—it's practically a guaranteed stop on the road you're traveling.

Let's break it down. When you're constantly striving for perfection, you're always running at full speed. Every task is high-stakes, every detail must be flawless, and there's no room for error. Sound exhausting? That's because it is. Perfectionism pushes you to keep going, even when you're tired, even when you've given everything you have—because there's always something that could be better, right?

But here's the catch: perfection doesn't exist. So, no matter how hard you push, you're never going to reach that finish line. And the longer you keep chasing it, the more worn out you become. Eventually, you hit a wall. That's burnout. It's what happens when your body and mind say, "Enough is enough," even though you're still convinced you could be doing more. The relentless pursuit of perfection finally catches up with you, and it's not pretty.

Burnout doesn't happen overnight. It creeps up on you slowly, like a leaky faucet you ignore until it turns into a flood. At first, it's just a bit of extra stress. You tell yourself you're fine, you can handle it. But then you start feeling more tired than usual, and tasks that used to excite you now feel like chores. You're snapping at people over little things, and no matter how much sleep you get, you wake up feeling drained. That's burnout knocking at your door.

Here's the thing about perfectionists: they're great at ignoring the signs of burnout. Why? Because they've convinced themselves that if they just work a little harder, push a little more, they can avoid feeling this way. But that's like trying to outrun a speeding train—it's not going to happen. The more you push yourself without taking a break, the faster burnout catches up. And once it does, you're stuck in a cycle of exhaustion that's hard to escape.

Burnout doesn't just affect your energy levels. It seeps into every area of your life. Suddenly, things that used to bring you joy feel like burdens. Your hobbies? Too tiring. Spending time with friends? Draining. Even getting out of bed in the morning feels like an Olympic sport. You start to lose your passion for the things that once made you excited, and that's when burnout really digs its claws in. The perfectionist drive that once fueled you is now burning you out, literally.

But what's really causing this burnout? Is it the tasks themselves? Probably not. It's the pressure you put on yourself to do everything perfectly, all the time. You're setting the bar so high that you're constantly stretching to reach it, and no one can sustain that pace forever. It's like running a marathon at sprint speed—you'll make it a few miles, but eventually, you're going to collapse.

So, how do you stop burnout before it takes over? First, you have to recognize that perfection isn't sustainable. (There's that word again—perfection!) You're not a machine; you're a human being, and human beings have limits. A huge part of avoiding burnout is accepting those limits and learning to work *within* them instead of constantly trying to break through them.

Think of it this way: imagine you're filling a glass of water. You keep pouring and pouring, but the glass can only hold so much before it overflows. That's what burnout is—your body and mind overflowing because you've poured in too much stress, too many demands, and not enough rest. If you don't stop to refill your energy, you'll end up with an empty glass, and that's not going to help anyone.

Another important step in avoiding burnout? Learn to say no. For perfectionists, saying no feels like admitting defeat, but it's actually a superpower. When you say no to tasks or commitments that are draining you, you're giving yourself the space to recharge. You don't have to be everything to everyone all the time. Prioritize what matters, and let go of the rest. The world won't fall apart, I promise.

And let's not forget about rest—because perfectionists are *really* bad at resting. You might think that taking a break is lazy or unproductive, but here's the truth: rest is just as important as work. Without it, you're running on fumes. Your mind and body need downtime to recover, recharge, and, you know, just *be*. If you're constantly on the go, burnout is inevitable. So, take that nap, read a book for fun, binge-watch your favorite show—whatever helps you unwind. You've earned it.

Here's the funny thing about burnout: it often strikes when you're right in the middle of trying to achieve something important. It's like the universe's way of saying, "Slow down, or you're going to crash." And when you crash, all that hard work you were doing? It goes out the window because you're too tired to finish it. So really, taking breaks and setting realistic goals isn't just about avoiding burnout—it's about *actually* getting things done in a sustainable way.

At the end of the day, the pursuit of perfection will never be worth the cost of burnout. Perfectionism might feel like the thing that's driving you to succeed, but in reality, it's draining you dry. The sooner you let go of the need to do everything perfectly, the sooner you can start living a life where you're not constantly exhausted and on edge. And trust me, that life feels a lot better.

Reflection Questions:

1. Have you ever experienced burnout because of your perfectionist tendencies? How did it affect your physical and emotional well-being?
2. How does the pressure to be perfect influence how much you take on in your daily life?
3. What would happen if you allowed yourself to take breaks without guilt, even if everything isn't "done" yet?
4. Can you identify the early warning signs of burnout in yourself? What steps can you take when you notice those signs?
5. How would it feel to set more realistic goals that prioritize your well-being instead of just your productivity?

Practical Exercise:

This week, set a "cut-off" time for your work or personal projects—at a reasonable hour. Once that time hits, stop working, no matter where you are in the process. Spend the rest of the evening resting, relaxing, or doing something you enjoy. Reflect on how taking this break affects your energy levels and productivity the next day.

Remember, you're not a machine—you're human. And humans need rest, balance, and realistic goals. Let go of the relentless pursuit of perfection and make room for the peace and joy that come with knowing when to take a step back. Your mind, body, and spirit will thank you.

Chapter 8: Avoidance of Feedback

Let's be real—feedback isn't always fun. In fact, if you're a perfectionist, feedback can feel like a punch to the gut. Why? Because it's often interpreted as a spotlight on your imperfections. And if there's one thing perfectionists hate, it's being reminded that they aren't perfect. You might find yourself avoiding feedback altogether or, when you do receive it, reacting defensively as if someone just insulted your entire existence. Sound familiar?

Here's the funny part: feedback is actually one of the most valuable tools for growth. It's like getting a roadmap to help you improve, learn, and become better at what you do. But when you're trapped in a perfectionist mindset, feedback doesn't feel like helpful advice—it feels like someone handing you a list of all your failures. And who wants to look at that, right?

But avoiding feedback comes at a cost. If you're constantly dodging it, you're missing out on opportunities to grow. Think about it like this: imagine you're building a piece of furniture without any instructions. Sure, you might figure it out on your own, but if someone handed you a guide with tips on how to do it better, wouldn't that make things easier? Feedback is that guide—it helps you see what you can't from your own perspective.

But perfectionists often don't want to hear it. Why? Because hearing that something isn't perfect feels like failure. You worked hard, you put in the effort, and now someone is telling you it wasn't quite right? Cue the internal meltdown. The problem isn't the feedback itself—it's how perfectionists interpret it. Instead of seeing feedback as a way to improve, it's viewed as confirmation of inadequacy. And that's a tough pill to swallow.

Here's a little secret: nobody's perfect (yeah, I know, you've heard that one before). But let's go a bit deeper—nobody *expects* you to be perfect either. The people giving you feedback aren't sitting there thinking, "Wow, this person should have done everything flawlessly." No, they're usually just trying to help. In fact, most people respect and appreciate those who are open to feedback because it shows a willingness to learn and improve.

So, why does feedback feel so personal to perfectionists? It's because perfectionism ties your self-worth to your achievements. When someone critiques your work, it can feel like they're criticizing *you*. Suddenly, it's not just about improving the task—it's about defending your very identity. And that's a lot of pressure to put on something like a suggestion to tweak your PowerPoint slides.

But what if feedback wasn't about judgment? What if it was about collaboration, about making something better together? Because here's the truth: feedback isn't an attack—it's a tool. And the people giving you feedback? They're not enemies; they're partners in your growth. When you can shift your mindset to see feedback as a gift (yeah, I said it—*a gift*), you'll start to realize how much it can help you become the person you want to be.

Let's take a step back. Think of a time when you received

feedback and immediately went into defense mode. Maybe you thought, "They don't get it," or "I knew it wasn't good enough." Now, ask yourself: Did that reaction help you improve? Did it make the feedback less valid? Probably not. In fact, getting defensive usually means you're so focused on protecting yourself that you miss the opportunity to learn.

Imagine this scenario: You're learning to cook, and you serve a meal to your friend. They tell you it's good but could use a little more seasoning. Now, you could take that feedback and feel insulted. "What? Are you saying I'm a terrible cook?" Or, you could hear it for what it is—helpful advice to make the next dish even better. Which approach will lead to tastier meals? (Hint: it's not the one where you throw the spatula down in frustration.)

The point is, feedback isn't the enemy. Your reaction to it is what turns it into something negative. When you start to see feedback as a tool rather than an indictment of your imperfections, you open the door to growth. And here's another kicker: the more you embrace feedback, the more confident you'll become. Why? Because feedback helps you get better, and getting better builds confidence. It's a win-win.

But what if the feedback isn't delivered in the nicest way? Well, that's another challenge. Not all feedback is sugar-coated, and sometimes it can feel harsh. But even then, there's usually something valuable to take away. The trick is to separate the delivery from the content. Maybe the person giving the feedback didn't say it as kindly as they could have, but if there's truth in it, that's where your focus should be. Don't throw out the whole message just because it wasn't wrapped in a bow.

So, how do you get better at accepting feedback without feeling like it's a personal attack? First, try to reframe how you see it. Instead of thinking, "This is proof that I'm not good enough," try thinking, "This is information that can help me improve." It's not about you as a person—it's about the task at hand. Second, practice gratitude. (I know, easier said than done.) But seriously, thank the people who take the time to give you feedback. They're investing in your growth, and that's something to appreciate.

Lastly, give yourself permission to not be perfect. When you let go of the idea that you have to get everything right all the time, feedback becomes less threatening. It's okay to make mistakes—it's part of the process. And remember, even the most successful people in the world got to where they are because they learned from their mistakes, not because they avoided them.

Reflection Questions:

1. How do you typically react to feedback? Do you get defensive or avoid it altogether? Why do you think that is?
2. Can you think of a time when feedback helped you improve, even if it was uncomfortable to hear at first?
3. What would change if you saw feedback as an opportunity to grow rather than a judgment on your abilities?
4. How do you feel when *you* give feedback to others? Do you expect them to be perfect, or do you appreciate their willingness to improve?
5. What steps can you take to embrace feedback more openly and with less fear of judgment?

Practical Exercise:

This week, seek out feedback on something you've been working on. It can be as small as asking a coworker how you did on a presentation or asking a friend for their thoughts on a personal project. When you receive the feedback, focus on listening without getting defensive or justifying your choices. Reflect on what you can take away from their suggestions and how it can help you improve.

Remember, feedback isn't there to tear you down—it's there to help build you up. The more you embrace it, the more you'll grow. So, next time someone offers you advice or criticism, try thanking them instead of cringing. You might be surprised at how much it changes your perspective.

Chapter 9: Obsession Over Mistakes

Let's face it, we all make mistakes. Big ones, small ones, embarrassing ones—mistakes are part of life. But for a perfectionist? Oh, no. Mistakes aren't just little hiccups; they're glaring neon signs flashing, "You failed!" And instead of letting those mistakes go, you might find yourself obsessing over them, replaying them in your head like a bad movie you can't turn off. If that sounds familiar, welcome to the world of perfectionist regret, where every misstep feels like a catastrophe.

Think about it—how often do you find yourself dwelling on something that went wrong? Maybe you said the wrong thing in a meeting, or you sent an email with a typo. Days, weeks, or even months later, it's still eating at you. You replay the scene in your mind, imagining all the ways it could have gone differently, wondering how people must have judged you. Sound familiar? For a perfectionist, mistakes aren't just moments—they're full-blown mental spirals.

Here's the thing: everyone makes mistakes. That's not just a cliché; it's a fact. But perfectionism tricks you into believing that mistakes are unacceptable, that they define your worth, and that they're proof you'll never be good enough. And so, instead of brushing them off and moving on, you zoom in on them like Sherlock Holmes, analyzing every little detail, as if by doing so, you can somehow fix the past. Spoiler alert: you can't.

But what happens when you obsess over your mistakes? You get stuck. It's like driving a car but only looking in the rearview mirror—you're not going anywhere, and you're missing every-thing happening around you. By focusing so much on what went wrong, you lose sight of the opportunities ahead of you. That job you didn't apply for because you messed up a presentation six months ago? That trip you didn't take because you booked the wrong hotel last time? You're letting your mistakes hold you back from new experiences, and that's a real shame.

Obsessing over mistakes also keeps you from seeing them for what they really are: learning opportunities. No one gets everything right the first time, and that's okay! But when you're stuck in perfectionist mode, mistakes feel like a dead end. You focus on the fact that you messed up, rather than on what you could learn from the situation. It's like tripping over a rock and then sitting there staring at the rock for hours, wondering why it was in your path, instead of just getting back up and continuing your walk.

But why do we do this to ourselves? Why does perfectionism make us so obsessed with mistakes? The answer is pretty simple: fear. Fear of failure, fear of judgment, fear of not measuring up. Perfectionists believe that if they make a mistake, it's a reflection of their worth. It's not just, "I made a mistake," but, "*I am* a mistake." And that's a heavy burden to carry.

So how do we break free from this obsession? First, it helps to remember that mistakes are not the enemy. They're a natural part of growth. In fact, some of the most successful people in the world got to where they are because of their mistakes—not in spite of them. Think about it: how do you learn to walk without falling? How do you master a new skill without messing up a few (or a hundred) times along the way? Mistakes are part of the process, not proof that you're a failure.

Next, you have to shift your focus. Instead of obsessing over what went wrong, try asking yourself, "What can I learn from this?" Every mistake has a lesson hidden in it, but you won't find it if you're too busy beating yourself up. Let's say you botched a work presentation. Sure, it wasn't your finest moment, but what could you do differently next time? Maybe you need to practice more, or maybe you realized that speaking in front of people isn't your thing. Either way, you've learned something valuable. And that's way more useful than just sitting around feeling guilty.

Here's another tip: remind yourself that people aren't as focused on your mistakes as you are. Really. You might think everyone is still talking about that awkward thing you said two months ago, but chances are, they've long forgotten it. People are far more concerned with their own lives and their own mistakes to dwell on yours. So, give yourself a break! The world isn't keeping score the way you are.

But what about those big mistakes—the ones that really hurt? The ones where you genuinely let someone down or made a decision you regret? Those are harder to let go of, right? In those cases, it's important to make amends where you can and then practice self-forgiveness. Yes, self-forgiveness. You're human, and humans mess up. What matters is that you learn from it, make things right if possible, and then—here's the key—move on. Carrying guilt forever doesn't help anyone, least of all yourself.

The real tragedy of obsessing over mistakes isn't the mistake itself—it's the fact that you stop moving forward. Life is full of opportunities, new challenges, and fresh starts, but you can't embrace them if you're always looking back. So, the next time you find yourself replaying a mistake in your mind, ask yourself, "Is this helping me?" If the answer is no, let it go. Because clinging to the past only keeps you from stepping into the future.

Reflection Questions:

1. What mistake are you currently dwelling on, and how is it preventing you from moving forward?
2. How would your life change if you saw mistakes as learning opportunities instead of personal failures?
3. Can you think of a time when someone else made a mistake and you easily forgave them? How can you apply that same forgiveness to yourself?
4. How does obsessing over past mistakes affect your confidence in trying new things?
5. What steps can you take to let go of a specific mistake and focus on future growth?

Practical Exercise:

Identify a mistake that's been bothering you recently. Write down what happened, how you felt about it, and, most importantly, what you've learned from it. Afterward, write down one action you can take to move forward from that mistake—whether it's forgiving yourself, making amends, or simply letting it go. Keep this exercise somewhere you can revisit it whenever you feel stuck in perfectionist regret.

Remember, mistakes don't define you. They shape you, guide you, and help you grow. The only real mistake is letting them stop you from moving forward. So, stop staring at the rock you tripped over—get back up and keep going. Your next adventure is waiting.

55

Chapter 10: Limited Creativity

Creativity is like a playground for your mind. It's where you get to explore, experiment, and express yourself without boundaries. Or at least, that's how it's *supposed* to be. But if you're a perfectionist, that playground can quickly feel more like a prison. Why? Because when your inner perfectionist is calling the shots, creativity gets stifled. You become so focused on making everything flawless that you're afraid to even start. After all, what if the result doesn't live up to your high standards? Better to play it safe, right?

Here's the thing: creativity and perfectionism don't play well together. Creativity is messy, unpredictable, and often requires a bit of trial and error. Perfectionism, on the other hand, demands structure, control, and the guarantee that whatever you create will be absolutely flawless. You can see the conflict, right? When you set impossibly high standards for yourself, creativity shrinks in the shadow of those expectations. Instead of feeling free to create, you feel paralyzed by the fear of not doing it perfectly.

Have you ever had a great idea for a project—whether it's painting, writing, cooking, or anything else creative—only to stop before you even begin because you're worried it won't turn out exactly as you imagined? That's perfectionism blocking your creative flow. It's like wanting to dive into a pool, but standing on the edge, frozen by the thought, "What if my dive isn't perfect?" Meanwhile, the water (your creativity) is just waiting for you to jump in and enjoy the experience.

The truth is, creativity *needs* imperfection. It thrives on experimentation and happy accidents. Think about some of the most famous works of art or innovation—they often didn't start as perfect visions. They evolved through trial and error, through the willingness to take risks and make mistakes. If every artist, writer, or inventor waited until they were sure their creation would be perfect before they started, we'd be missing out on a lot of masterpieces.

So, what does perfectionism do to your creativity? It traps it. Instead of letting your ideas flow freely, you put them under a microscope, examining every detail before you even start. You tell yourself things like, "It has to be perfect or it's not worth doing," or "What if people don't like it?" And just like that, your creative energy gets squashed before it even has a chance to take off. The fear of imperfection becomes a brick wall between you and your creative potential.

Here's the irony: perfectionists often admire creative people. You might look at a painter or a musician or a writer and think, "Wow, I wish I could be that free with my creativity." But guess what? Those people aren't immune to mistakes. They've just learned to embrace them. They know that not everything they create will be perfect—and they're okay with that. They understand that creativity is more about the process than the end result. And if you can adopt that mindset, you'll find that your creativity starts to bloom.

Let's talk about the creative process for a minute. Creativity isn't a straight line from A to B. It's more like a winding path with a few detours, some dead ends, and a lot of unexpected surprises along the way. Sometimes, what you create doesn't turn out the way you planned—and that's okay! In fact, some of the best creative work comes from the unplanned moments. But if you're too focused on perfection, you miss those opportunities. You're too busy worrying about what *should* be, instead of letting yourself enjoy what *could* be.

Perfectionism also tends to put a time limit on creativity. You might tell yourself, "If I don't get this right on the first try, I'm not good at it," or "If it takes too long to perfect, it's not worth doing." But creativity doesn't work on a schedule. Some ideas take time to develop. Some projects need a few rounds of trial and error before they start to come together. If you rush the process or demand immediate perfection, you're cutting your creativity off at the knees.

Here's a little exercise: think back to a time when you allowed yourself to be creative without worrying about the outcome. Maybe you doodled in a notebook during class, wrote a silly story as a kid, or just tried a new recipe for fun. Remember how freeing that felt? That's what creativity is supposed to feel like— playful, experimental, and most of all, fun. But perfectionism takes the fun out of it. It turns a joyful process into a stressful one, where the focus is on getting everything right instead of enjoying the act of creating.

So, how do you break free from the perfectionism trap and reclaim your creativity? First, give yourself permission to make mistakes. Seriously, say it out loud if you need to: "I give myself permission to create something imperfect." When you let go of the need for everything to be flawless, you'll find that your creative energy starts flowing again. You'll feel more open to trying new things, experimenting with different ideas, and taking risks. And that's when the magic happens.

Second, focus on the process, not the product. Creativity is a journey, not a destination. Whether you're painting a canvas, writing a story, or trying out a new recipe, remind yourself that the value is in the doing, not just in the finished result. Even if what you create isn't "perfect" (whatever that means), you've still learned something, had fun, and expressed yourself—and that's what creativity is all about.

Finally, set realistic expectations for your creative projects. Instead of demanding perfection, set a goal to simply *start* something. Tell yourself, "I'm going to write for 10 minutes," or "I'll paint one small section of this canvas." Take the pressure off, and see what happens when you approach creativity with curiosity instead of judgment. You might be surprised at what you come up with when you're not trying so hard to get everything right.

At the end of the day, perfectionism is a creativity killer. It's the voice that says, "Don't bother unless it's perfect." But creativity doesn't need perfection. It needs freedom, flexibility, and a willingness to embrace the unknown. So, the next time you feel that perfectionist voice creeping in, remind yourself that creativity is messy—and that's a good thing. Let go, dive in, and see where your imagination takes you.

Reflection Questions:

1. Can you recall a time when perfectionism stopped you from starting or finishing a creative project? How did that feel?
2. How would it feel to create something without worrying about whether it's perfect?
3. What's one creative activity you've always wanted to try

but haven't because you're afraid of not being good at it?
4. How do you define creativity, and how has perfectionism shaped that definition?
5. What's the worst that could happen if you created something imperfect? What's the best that could happen?

Practical Exercise:

Choose a creative activity you've been avoiding because of perfectionist fears. Set a timer for 20 minutes and commit to working on it during that time—without worrying about how good the final product is. Whether it's writing, drawing, playing music, or something else, focus only on the act of creating, not the result. At the end of the 20 minutes, reflect on how it felt to create without the pressure of perfection.

Remember, creativity isn't about getting everything right—it's about expressing yourself, trying new things, and having fun along the way. Perfection can wait. Let your imagination take the lead.

Now WHAT? You May Ask.

So, you've come this far. You've read about how perfectionism creeps into different areas of your life—whether it's making you anxious, stopping you from taking opportunities, or even suffocating your creativity. And now you might be wondering: *Now what?* Where do you go from here? How do you actually start to make changes and live life without the weight of perfectionism constantly hanging over your head?

The first step is acknowledging that change doesn't happen overnight. This isn't a quick fix, and that's okay. After all, you didn't become a perfectionist in a day, so you're not going to undo those habits in a day either. But don't let that discourage you. The real question is: *What's the alternative?* Would you rather stay stuck in the exhausting cycle of trying to meet impossible standards, or would you prefer to begin letting go and start living with more freedom?

You see, the path forward isn't about suddenly becoming carefree or pretending that you don't care about doing well. It's about shifting your mindset. Instead of thinking, "This has to be perfect," try asking, "What can I learn from this?" or "How can I grow from this experience?" Once you start to see life as a series of learning opportunities, rather than tests you have to ace, things become a lot less intimidating. Doesn't that sound a little more manageable?

But let's get real—this shift in thinking won't be automatic. There will be days when the perfectionist inside you screams, "You're not good enough!" and tries to convince you that any slip-up is catastrophic. And on those days, the most important thing you can do is take a deep breath and remind yourself that mistakes are not failures—they're part of the process. Here's a question to consider: *When was the last time you truly learned something new without making any mistakes along the way?* Probably never. So why do you expect perfection from yourself every time?

As you move forward, one of the best things you can do is practice being kind to yourself. I know, it sounds cliché, but self-compassion is a game-changer. Instead of beating yourself up when things don't go perfectly, try talking to yourself the way you would talk to a friend. If your friend messed up, you wouldn't say, "Wow, you really blew it. You should've been perfect!" No, you'd reassure them, remind them it's okay, and encourage them to keep going. So why not offer yourself the same kindness?

Now, I can hear you thinking: *But what if I stop holding myself to high standards? Won't I just start slacking off?* This is a common fear, but here's the truth—letting go of perfectionism doesn't mean letting go of excellence. You can still aim to do well without demanding perfection. In fact, you might discover that you perform better when you stop worrying about every little detail and give yourself some breathing room. This is because fear won't paralyze you. The question to ask yourself is: *What's more important—being perfect or making progress?*

Another thing to consider is that you don't have to go through this alone. Whether it's opening up to friends or family about your perfectionist tendencies or seeking out support from a therapist or mentor, talking about your struggles can be incredibly freeing. You might be surprised at how many people around you are dealing with the same feelings. Remember, perfectionism thrives in silence. When you start to open up, you take away some of its power. So, who can you reach out to for support?

Of course, as you start to work through your perfectionism, there will still be challenges. Life is messy, and that's part of what makes it beautiful. There will be days when things don't go according to plan—when you stumble, fall, or make mistakes. But here's a thought: *What if you saw those moments not as failures, but as opportunities for growth?* What if every misstep was a step toward becoming stronger, wiser, and more resilient? Wouldn't that change how you approach the unknown?

At this point, you might be thinking, *Okay, I get it. But how do I actually put this into practice?* Start small. You don't need to overhaul your entire life in one go. Begin by setting realistic goals, ones that don't require perfection but focus on progress. Allow yourself to be a little more flexible in how you approach tasks. If something doesn't go perfectly, let it go and move on, rather than letting it define your day. Ask yourself, *What's one small area of my life where I can loosen my grip on perfection?*

The truth is, life isn't a test you pass or fail. It's an experience to be lived, complete with ups, downs, mistakes, and surprises. And the morc you let go of the need to do everything perfectly, the more you'll open yourself up to new possibilities, new joys, and—most importantly—new ways of being your best, *imperfect* self. Because here's the thing: *Perfection isn't where your value lies. Your value comes from who you are, how you grow, and how you connect with the world around you.*

So, now what? You start where you are, with what you have. You take one small step toward letting go of perfectionism, and then another, and another. You remind yourself that you're not on this journey to be perfect—you're on it to grow, to learn, and to live more fully. You embrace the messiness, the mistakes, and the unknown. And as you do, you'll discover something amazing: *Life is a lot more fun when you stop trying to make it perfect.*

Reflection Questions:

1. In what areas of your life do you feel perfectionism holding you back the most?
2. How would your life change if you embraced progress over perfection?
3. What's one mistake you've made recently, and what lesson can you take from it?
4. How do you think your relationships would improve if you stopped expecting perfection from yourself and others?
5. What's the smallest step you can take today to start letting go of your perfectionist tendencies?

Practical Exercise:

Choose one task or area of your life where perfectionism tends to sneak in. This week, make a conscious effort to focus on progress rather than perfection. Whether it's a work project, a creative hobby, or even a conversation with a friend, set a goal to simply start and make progress—without worrying about getting it exactly right. At the end of the week, reflect on how this approach felt and what you learned from letting go of perfection.

Remember, life isn't perfect—and neither are you. And that's exactly what makes it, and you, so wonderfully unique.

65

Conclusion: Embrace Your Imperfections

Congratulations! You've made it to the end of this book, and what a journey it's been. Whether you started this book because you wanted to stop feeling like perfection was constantly looming over you, or you were just curious about how to make life a little easier and more enjoyable, I hope you've found some valuable insights here. More importantly, I hope you're walking away with a new perspective—one that reminds you that *you don't have to be perfect to be amazing.*

Perfectionism is tough. It sneaks into our thoughts, our habits, and our lives in ways that can be hard to shake. But the fact that you've come this far shows that you're ready to make a change. You're ready to embrace the fact that mistakes are part of growth, that progress is better than perfection, and that letting go of those impossible standards doesn't mean letting go of your desire to succeed—it just means living with more peace, joy, and self-compassion.

As you go forward, I want you to remember this: the pursuit of perfection is not the path to happiness, success, or fulfillment. Real happiness comes from being kind to yourself, from learning and growing through your experiences, and from accepting that life's messiness is what makes it beautiful. You don't need to be flawless to be worthy, and you don't need to have it all figured out to move forward.

Thank you for buying and reading this book. I know your time is valuable, and I'm truly grateful that you chose to spend it with me and these ideas. I hope what you've read here will help you not only let go of perfectionism but also live a life that feels fuller, more joyful, and a little lighter.

If you found this book helpful, I'd love to ask a small favor: *please consider leaving a review.* Your review won't just help me—it'll help other readers who might be struggling with the same perfectionist tendencies you've faced. By sharing your thoughts, you're helping spread this message to people who need to hear it. You're letting others know that it's okay to embrace imperfection, stop chasing impossible standards, and live life more freely.

So, if you've got a moment, I'd truly appreciate it if you could share your review of this book. It could make all the difference for someone who's looking for the encouragement and tools to break free from perfectionism, just like you have.

Thank you again for reading, and remember: you're already enough, just as you are.

All my best,

Yakalou

www.ingramcontent.com/pod-product-compliance
Lightning Source LLC
Chambersburg PA
CBHW061307250726
48653CB00002B/827